VIRGO

August 23 – September 22

Christine Webster

www.av2books.com

Step 1
Go to **www.av2books.com**

Step 2
Enter this unique code
PEJUXSYAL

Step 3
Explore your interactive eBook!

AV2 is optimized for use on any device

Your interactive eBook comes with...

Contents
Browse a live contents page to easily navigate through resources

Audio
Listen to sections of the book read aloud

Videos
Watch informative video clips

Weblinks
Gain additional information for research

Try This!
Complete activities and hands-on experiments

Key Words
Study vocabulary, and complete a matching word activity

Quizzes
Test your knowledge

Slideshows
View images and captions

... and much, much more!

VIRGO

August 23 – September 22

Contents

Are You a Virgo?

Do people describe you as a kind person? Are you interested in animals and nature? If this sounds familiar, you may be a Virgo. A Virgo is someone who was born between August 23 and September 22.

Virgo is a sign in the zodiac. This is a series of 12 **constellations** that run across the night sky. For centuries, people have used these groups of stars to tell the future. The study of the stars in this manner is called astrology.

Zodiac Chart

A person's zodiac sign is determined by his or her date of birth. Which sign matches your birthday?

It's in the Stars

The zodiac constellations form a circle around Earth. In one year, Earth makes a full **orbit** around the Sun. As it does this, the Sun appears to be in different places at set times. The zodiac constellations are found along the path the Sun follows.

Long ago, people used the Sun to tell the time of year. In late August, the Sun passed through the Virgo constellation. People born then were said to be born under the sign of Virgo.

Over time, the position of the constellations shifted. Even though the Sun now passes through Virgo at a different time, the dates associated with the sign of Virgo remain the same.

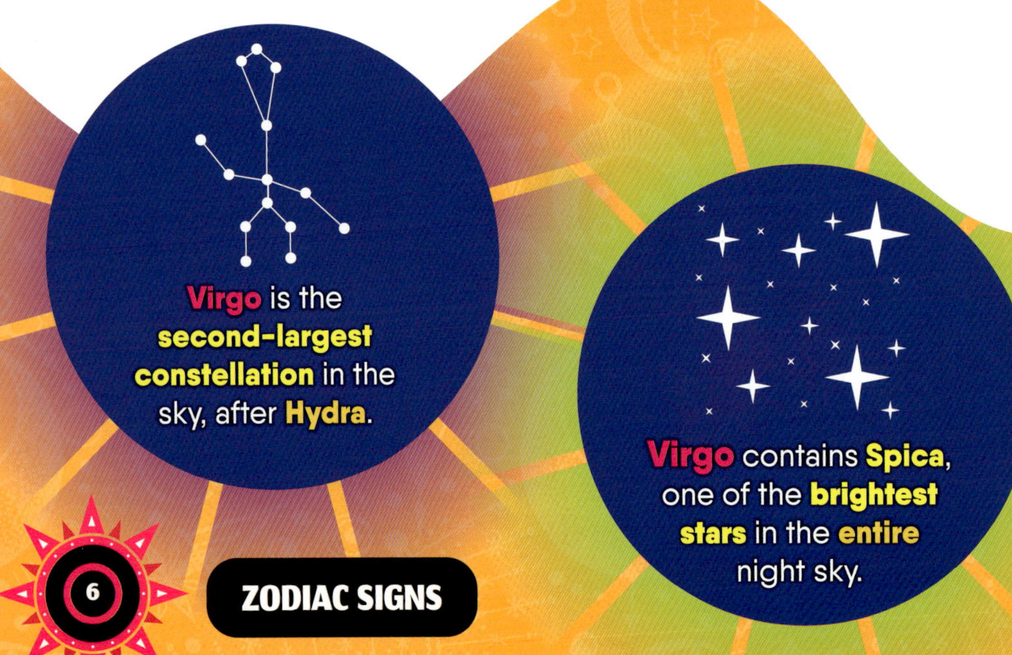

Virgo is the largest of all the zodiac constellations.

The Myth of Virgo

The ancient Greeks had stories about how each zodiac constellation came to be in the sky. Virgo is linked to the Greek goddess Persephone, maiden of spring.

Persephone was the daughter of Demeter, the **harvest** goddess, and Zeus, the father of men and gods. At one time, Earth was in a state of constant spring. This changed when Hades, god of the **underworld**, kidnapped the spring maiden.

Demeter was devastated by the loss of Persephone, and cursed the fields in grief. Unless mother and daughter were reunited, Earth would bear no fruit. Zeus demanded that Hades bring Persephone back. However, while in the underworld, Persephone had eaten some pomegranate seeds. This prevented her from returning permanently to Earth.

Persephone was allowed to return to Earth for part of the year, but was forced to spend the rest of the year underground. This is why spring now lasts for only a short time, when the constellation Virgo can be seen in the night sky above the horizon.

Persephone was the queen of the underworld. She ruled alongside her husband, Hades.

Virgo and Mutable Signs

In astrology, some zodiac signs share certain **qualities**. These qualities show how a person acts in the world. The qualities are separated into three groups. Cardinal signs are known for being **trendsetters**. Fixed signs make ideas come to life. Mutable signs deal with change easily.

Virgo is a mutable sign. People in this group are known for being comfortable with life changes. They are more flexible than other signs. Mutable signs can easily adapt to any situation. They are also very intelligent.

Mutable signs pay attention to detail.

Zodiac Signs
by Quality

Cardinal Signs
Are known for being trendsetters.

Aries

Cancer

Libra

Capricorn

Fixed Signs
Make ideas come to life.

Taurus

Leo

Scorpio

Aquarius

Mutable Signs
Deal with change easily.

Gemini

Virgo

Sagittarius

Pisces

Virgo as an Earth Sign

Zodiac signs are also grouped according to the four **classical elements**. These are fire, earth, water, and air. Signs that belong to the same group share common personality traits.

Virgo is an earth sign. Earth people often feel a strong sense of **duty**. They are known for being reliable. Earth people can also be very practical and grounded. This helps them avoid taking risks.

Earth people are known as the builders of the zodiac.

Zodiac Signs
by Element

Fire

Aries

Leo

Sagittarius

Earth

Taurus

Virgo

Capricorn

Air

Gemini

Libra

Aquarius

Water

Cancer

Scorpio

Pisces

Being a Virgo

A Virgo's earth traits and mutable qualities combine to create a specific type of person. A key Virgo strength is having a strong work ethic. Virgos are incredibly hard workers. They finish any job they start to the best of their ability.

Virgos have their weaknesses as well. They love to improve themselves. While not a bad quality in itself, this may cause them to overthink. Sometimes, Virgos care too much about the opinions of other people. This can cause Virgos to become distressed.

Virgo is ruled by the planet **Mercury**. It takes Mercury **88 days** to complete a **single orbit** around the **Sun**.

Wednesday is the **luckiest** day of the week for **Virgos**.

Virgos are known as critical thinkers. This helps them perfect their work.

Virgos through Time

Virgos have had a significant impact on the world over time. They have ruled nations, won Olympic medals, and made scientific breakthroughs. Their contributions have helped make the world what it is today.

British royal **Elizabeth I** (born September 7, 1533) becomes queen of England and Ireland at the age of 25.

Scientist **John Dalton** (born September 6, 1766) publishes the first volume of *A New System of Chemical Philosophy*, which outlines his **atomic theory**.

Track and field star **Jesse Owens** (born September 12, 1913) competes in the Berlin Olympics, winning four gold medals.

1954

Author **William Golding** (born September 19, 1911) publishes his first novel, the classic *Lord of the Flies*.

1961

Mathematician **Katherine Johnson** (born August 26, 1918) helps send the first U.S. crewed flight into space with her calculations.

2020

Professional basketball player **Kobe Bryant** (born August 23, 1978) is selected to be **posthumously** inducted into the Naismith Memorial Basketball Hall of Fame.

Making Friends

Some people believe that zodiac signs can help people form relationships. Each sign has its own traits. These traits can be a good fit with other signs. A Virgo might know ahead of time if someone would be a good friend just by finding out his or her sign.

It's Friendship

It's Love

Virgos often find romance with these signs.

Taurus

Cancer

Capricorn

It's Complicated

Gemini

Sagittarius

Leo

Virgos find it difficult to form bonds with these signs.

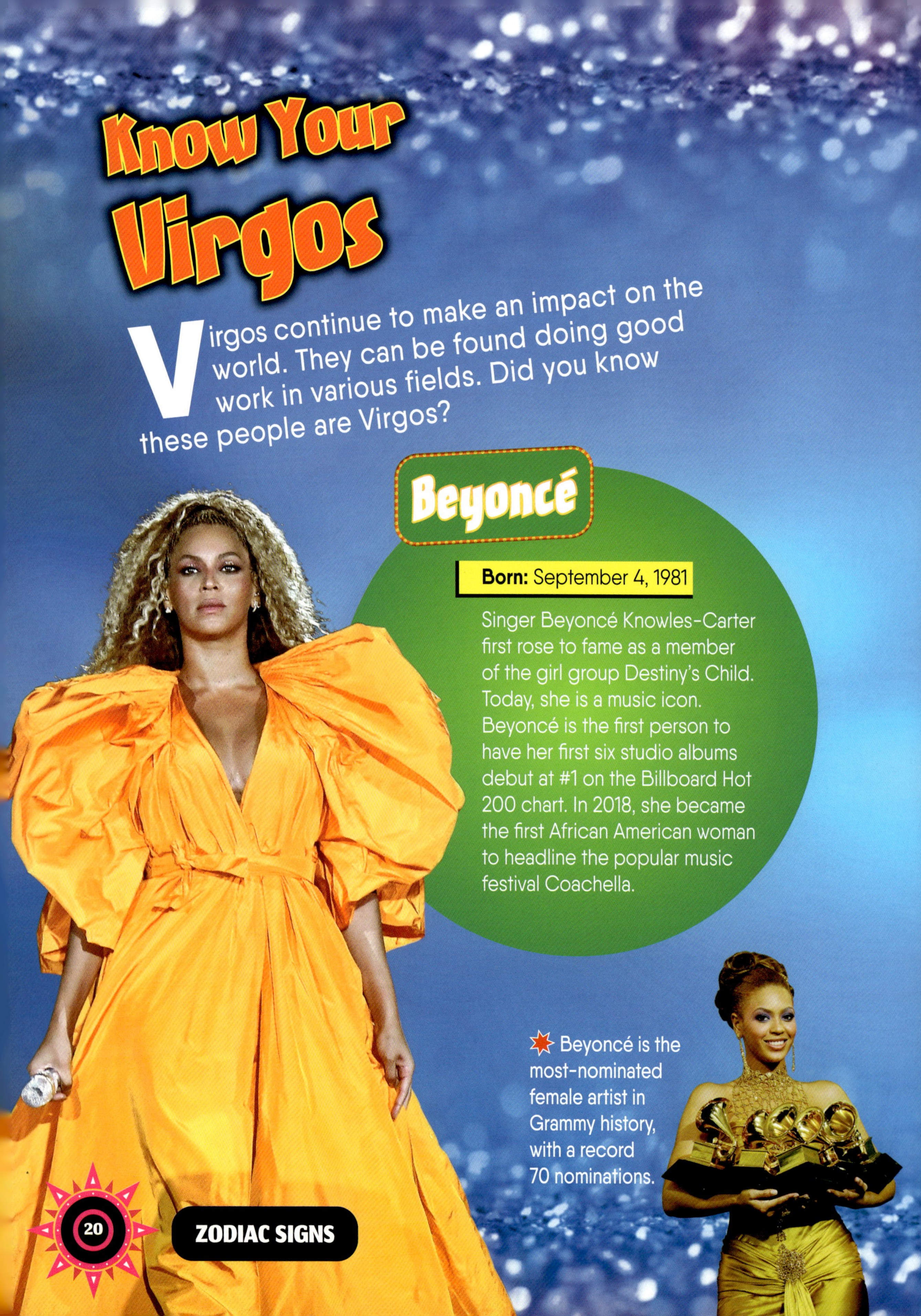

Know Your Virgos

Virgos continue to make an impact on the world. They can be found doing good work in various fields. Did you know these people are Virgos?

Beyoncé

Born: September 4, 1981

Singer Beyoncé Knowles-Carter first rose to fame as a member of the girl group Destiny's Child. Today, she is a music icon. Beyoncé is the first person to have her first six studio albums debut at #1 on the Billboard Hot 200 chart. In 2018, she became the first African American woman to headline the popular music festival Coachella.

Beyoncé is the most-nominated female artist in Grammy history, with a record 70 nominations.

Alexander Ovechkin

Born: September 17, 1985

Russian hockey player Alex Ovechkin began his National Hockey League (NHL) career in 2005. He quickly made his mark, scoring 52 goals in his first season. Alex is one of the greatest goal scorers ever, with eight 50-goal seasons to date.

Zendaya

Born: September 1, 1996

Actress Zendaya Maree Stoermer Coleman first became known for starring on the Disney show *Shake It Up*. Since then, she has written a book and launched her own clothing line. Zendaya also hit new heights of fame as MJ in the most recent Spider-Man franchise.

Prince Harry

Born: September 15, 1984

Prince Harry is the grandson of Queen Elizabeth II, the longest-ruling monarch in British history. He is sixth in line to the throne. Harry and his wife Meghan are well known for their charity work around the world. In 2020, they announced a new non-profit entity called Archewell.

Jimmy Fallon

Born: September 19, 1974

Jimmy Fallon is a comedian and television host. He first became famous for his impressions on *Saturday Night Live*, where he was a cast member for six seasons. In 2009, Jimmy hosted his own late-night talk show. He became the host of *The Tonight Show* in 2014.

The Virgo QUIZ

1 With which signs do Virgos find it difficult to form bonds?

2 Which celebrity Virgo first rose to fame in a girl group?

3 To which element group do Virgos belong?

4 Which planet rules Virgo?

5 What key strength do Virgos possess?

6 What sport does Virgo Alex Ovechkin play?

7 When did Virgo John Dalton publish his atomic theory?

8 Is a Virgo a cardinal, fixed, or mutable sign?

ANSWERS: 1. Gemini, Sagittarius, and Leo 2. Beyoncé 3. Earth 4. Mercury 5. A strong work ethic 6. Hockey 7. 1808 8. Mutable

Key Words

atomic theory: a scientific theory stating that all matter is made of indivisible building blocks called atoms

classical elements: materials from which all other materials were once believed to be made

constellations: groups of stars that form patterns in the sky

duty: responsibility or obligation

harvest: the time of year when crops are ready to be picked

orbit: a regular, repeating path that one object in space takes around another

posthumously: after a person's death

qualities: traits that make something what it is

trendsetters: people who lead the way with their ideas

underworld: a mythical place where souls are said to go after death

Index

Get the best of both worlds.

AV2 bridges the gap between print and digital.

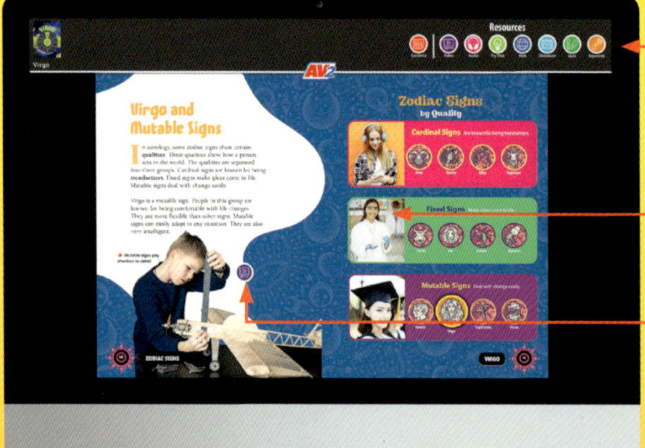

The expandable resources toolbar enables quick access to content including **videos**, **audio**, **activities**, **weblinks**, **slideshows**, **quizzes**, and **key words**.

Animated videos make static images come alive.

Resource icons on each page help readers to further **explore key concepts**.

Published by AV2
14 Penn Plaza 9th Floor
New York, NY 10122
Website: www.av2books.com

Library of Congress Control Number: 2020938527

ISBN 978-1-7911-2636-0 (hardcover)
ISBN 978-1-7911-2637-7 (softcover)
ISBN 978-1-7911-2638-4 (multi-user eBook)
ISBN 978-1-7911-2639-1 (single-user eBook)

Printed in Guangzhou, China
1 2 3 4 5 6 7 8 9 0 24 23 22 21 20

062020
101119

Editor: Katie Gillespie
Art Director: Terry Paulhus

Every reasonable effort has been made to trace ownership and to obtain permission to reprint copyright material. The publisher would be pleased to have any errors or omissions brought to their attention so that they may be corrected in subsequent printings.

AV2 acknowledges Getty Images, Alamy, iStock, and Shutterstock as its primary image suppliers for this title.